"I am filled with such a lovely presence each time I read these words. They connect me to an inner voice often drowned out by the daily noise."
   Tiffany Hall - Kinesiologist

"Most of us yearn for a daily practice that will center our hearts and minds for the day ahead. You'll find such a practice here, with just enough encouraging, poetic words to start you off. These are followed with time for silent meditation plus a place for you to write your own guiding words for the day. So, open this book and let it guide you to your own nurturing practice."
   Seena B. Frost - Creator of the SoulCollage® process and author of *SoulCollage® Evolving: An Intuitive Collage Process for Self-Discovery & Community*

Soul Infusions are portals through which you can deepen your awareness of the sacred and allow your love and vitality to flow freely into every area of your life. These 36 meditative poems create an oasis of refreshment that invites you to rest in the healing, transformative waters of your soul and allow spirit to gracefully bless your body, mind and heart.

These nuggets of wisdom offer a wealth of no-frills spiritual insight. They are uplifting, innocent, intimate and practical. You can use the prayers, individually or as a group, as avenues of inspiration to help you awaken to your natural wisdom and authentic expression.

"This is a lovely book. Heart-warming, soul-warming, life-warming. Engaging with it will connect you with grace and infuse you with joy."
   Mary Inglis - Long-term resident of the Findhorn Community, Partner InnerLinks Associates UK, Trainer, Coach.

"As a long-time player of the Transformation® Game, I have incorporated the Angels of the Game into my daily spiritual practice. The invocations in *Soul Infusions* create a powerful framework for adding another dimension to support my evolving relationship with Spirit. I would like to thank the Angel of 'Joy' for her inspired work."
   Heather Vaughn - Accredited Transformation® Game Facilitator.

What I love best about Joy is her willingness and courage to live up to her name. These beautiful soul songs, and her suggestions for exploring them, arise from her direct engagement with her own life's challenges. Joy offers us nuggets of gold that have been through the alchemy of deep earth fires to emerge as radiant wisdom. We can trust them as allies to guide us into our own fiery hope.
   Rue Anne Hass, M.A. - Author of *Opening the Cage of Pain with EFT, This is Where I Stand* and *The 8 Master Keys To Healing What Hurts*

Soul Infusions

Weaving Our Soul's Light Into The Fabric Of Every Day

Kristuia,
May the love that
inspired this book
lighten, brighten and
enliven your journey*
Many blessings!
Joy
Asheville
2016

Living Prayers & Daily Applications
Inspired at the Findhorn Foundation

Joy Drake

Soul Infusions:
Weaving Our Soul's Light Into The Fabric Of Every Day

Thanks to:
Gail Jolley for proofreading the text
Jeremy Berg for the front cover painting
Bonnie Cooper for the author picture
and the back cover Sunrise Panel photograph
bonniecooperphotography@yahoo.com Asheville, NC.

Sunrise Panel is the property of the Findhorn Foundation, Scotland.
Used with permission.

ISBN: 978-0-936878-69-0

Drake, Joy
Soul Infusions: *Weaving Our Soul's Light Into The Fabric Of Every Day*/Joy Drake

First Edition May 2015

Published by Lorian Press
686 Island View Dr
Camano Island, WA 98282

Dedication

Dedicated to all the big picture holders,
especially the Game Deva who steered me
as far away as possible from the straight and narrow.

Acknowledgements

This book has been steeping/infusing in my soul's creative pipeline for years, and its emergence has been shepherded and blessed by many helpers.

Thanks to the people who lived at the Findhorn Foundation when I was there and whose interactions with me brought the mystery school to life and contributed to my growth and spiritual awareness. Heartfelt thanks to the Findhorn Angel for giving me opportunities to serve that expressed my uniqueness and creativity to the fullest and beyond.

I'm incredibly grateful to friends who read early drafts, offered helpful comments, and encouraged me to keep writing; Dorothy Maclean, Mike Scott, Lynn Pace, Nancy Kehr, Tiffany Hall, Karen Luke Jackson, Kelly McKibben, Trey Carland and Lisa Koger.

Special thanks to Gail Jolley for her fine editing skills, even-mindedness and wisdom, to Joshua Heartsong for his inspiring companionship, and to my amazing son, Damien Drake, for his huge heart, wellspring of talents, and the many gifts he and his family bring me.

Deep thanks to my co-adventurers and life-long friends Kathy Tyler and Mary Inglis who, when I would timidly ask "But who am I to say anything?" would chorus "You're you, Joy!" Thank you for so lovingly and humorously helping me weave the transcendent into the fabric of my life. Your incredible friendship has enriched my journey immeasurably.

And, finally, never-ending gratitude to the Emerging Impulse for flinging me into the present moment with such passionate aliveness and style, and for gifting me with a wild new beginning.

Soul Infusion

is a journey of waking up and becoming
more aware of who you are,
what you are doing,
and why and how you are doing it.

It's about rooting ourselves
in the emerging consciousness and
transforming a series of unexpected experiences
into a playground for the sacred.

Contents

Origins and Development i
Crockpot Spirituality ii
Suggestions for Use iii
Getting Started iv

New Beginnings - Angel of Adventure 1

    1: a whole new world
    2: engage with life
    3: first class of the day
    4: here is your present
    5: rhythms of the sacred
    6: stay open
    7: step out
    8: strengthen your commitment
    9: we are infinite beings

Uniquely Alive! - Angel of Authenticity 21

    10: are you living a spiritual life?
    11: boldly go
    12: illuminating your way
    13: joy of living
    14: let go
    15: precision flying
    16: release the old
    17: unifying presence
    18: unwrapping

Activating Change - Angel of Transformation 41

19: affirmations of love
20: dare to love
21: it's up to you
22: our pledge to spirit
23: paradise now
24: soaking in grace
25: soul sight
26: spring cleaning
27: warriorship 101

Liberating Practices - Angel of Presence 61

28: all our meetings
29: filled with gratitude
30: here and now
31: into the new
32: let spirit flow
33: our hearts speak
34: voyage into light
35: we are here to love
36: with each breath

Beyond Our Lines 81
Afterword 82
Index of First Lines 83

Origins and Development

In my mid 20's I committed to be of service. Within short order I ended up at the Findhorn Foundation in the north of Scotland where I lived for fourteen years, 1971-1986. I particularly loved spending time in the Cluny Hill sanctuary. In the peace and quiet there I developed deep lasting inner connections that have helped shape my path of creativity and joyful service.

During the years 1975-79, I volunteered to lead a meditation in the sanctuary every Monday morning. There were about 30 community members living at Cluny Hill at that time and a new wave of guests arrived each Saturday to participate in workshops offered by the Foundation. Since the visitors came from many different spiritual backgrounds, it was important that the sanctuary readings not only touched their hearts, but also reflected clearly the values and orientation of the community.

The opening reading was a short invocation that set the tone and focused the group's energy. Then we spent about 15 minutes in meditation and closed with a blessing that released the energies generated to the world. I felt privileged to be part of the sanctuary team and opened fully to what wanted to be shared, giving my creative writing free rein.

My aim in writing these 'Sanctuaries' each week was to express the transcendent in no-frills, ordinary language. I wanted it to be true to the original divine impulse, to my personal experiences, and to all that inspired people to be their best.

I wanted to give human voice to the impulses of spirit as they flowed to me and through me. I also wanted to support the Cluny family and our guests in making deep inner connections and in applying spiritual principles and realizations to their relationships and in their work, so that these interactions and everyday environments could become as spiritually nourishing and expansive as the sanctuary, and thereby transformed.

At the time most of these meditations were written I was in my 30's. After reaching the prestigious heights of core group and management, I had voluntarily returned to the shop floor and was managing the Cluny Hill dining room. I was passionate about this work and my latest hobby, The Transformation Game. Looking back I can see how all three threads - the dining room, the Game, and the Sanctuaries - balanced and enhanced one another and provided an energetic loom on which spirit could weave the transcendent into and through the creative expressions of my life.

This was a radical and tumultuous time of awakening for the community. We all sensed that something utterly new and worthwhile was coming into form. These Sanctuaries reflect this exciting era in my own and the community's life.

Crockpot Spirituality:
Really Slow Cooking

When I left the Findhorn Foundation in the mid 80's to develop the boxed version of The Transformation Game, I had 36 'Sanctuaries' saved in a folder. Occasionally I'd pull one out and share it with a group I was leading or use it as an inspirational prompt in my spiritual practice, and then tuck it away again.

Then about ten years ago the Sanctuaries began calling to me, and the idea of writing a practical application for each guided meditation took hold. As I followed this impulse I felt the enthusiasm of the muses intertwining with my own open heart, blessing and enhancing what I felt excited about.

I began by reading a Sanctuary prayer out loud to focus my morning meditation. I'd repeat this with the same theme for a week or so, staying open to all that life brought my way that day, then outline some possible applications on the page opposite the meditation. This broadened the theme so that it brought wonder and willingness into the everyday and made the spiritual work a practical reality.

In response to my prayers, synchronicities were abundant. It was as if the universe were conspiring to animate the essence of each theme in ways I could not miss seeing. However the flow was erratic and most of the applications remained unfinished until last summer when I freed my schedule so I could resume the work I'd started almost forty years earlier!

I established a variety of rhythms to help me create a focused space and keep the work fresh and new. After choosing an Angel Card quality for the day I'd gaze at a collage I'd made to honor the Cluny Sanctuary. This made it easy to slide into a seat there in my imagination and drink in its energy. I'd stay until I felt the silence flow in and around me. Then I'd ask if the Sanctuary or my Angel for the day had a message or any advice to offer me. Their combined presence felt like my personal conduit to divine guidance.

Next I'd select one of the prayers and read it out loud imagining that I was sitting in the Cluny Sanctuary meditating with a group of guests. Then, after the closing blessing, the visualization would recede and I'd begin to write. I wrote each application in longhand first. It felt old fashioned and quill-like and slowed me down, which I liked a lot. If no words came I'd either move on to another theme or do something completely different like cleaning or cooking, while keeping my intuition tuned into the theme's frequency.

When phrases or snippets of conversations caught my attention I'd add them to the application and see what came next. Each time a sentence or paragraph completed itself it felt as if the muses were blessing this work, and my heart overflowed with deep gratitude and a wordsmith's delight.

As I surrendered to what I loved, life empowered the process. The co-creative forces used what I knew and gave me what it knew. The more I trusted my own source and allowed myself to be exactly who I was, the more the divine words flowed. I felt connected with the divine in everything. I felt able to give voice to it and bring it into expression.

As an agent of blessing I felt deeply blessed.

Suggestions for Use

Although originally written for group meditation, the prayers are easily adapted for individual use. Each theme spans two pages. On the left-hand page an invocation and blessing prayer guides the listener(s) into and out of meditation. Read them out loud, from your heart, even if you're alone. Feel their poetic, free-form, intuitive, inspirational, and universal nature.

On the right-hand page are suggestions for ways you can translate the meditation into action. Each application offers a few questions or a short vignette to help you get out of your own way so the theme of the meditation fully lands, roots and expresses in you. Some of the application pages have been left open for you to fill as you like with images or realizations. The suggestions are action oriented, personal, provocative and practical. Sometimes confronting, other times comforting, they are always loving and truthful. In group/retreat settings, the applications provide a variety of talking points that can inspire new conversations and discussions.

Neither of the two parts is complete or balanced without the other. It is one thing to talk about soul infusion and another to live as a soul-infused personality 24/7. If you feel you have a glorious spiritual life yet your house, family or work relationships are conflicted, miserable or in chaos, you have some human homework to do! It is my hope that incorporating these Sanctuaries into your spiritual practice will help you recognize and bridge any gaps.

A theme for each meditation is on the upper left of the page. I have grouped the prayers into four sections; New Beginnings, Uniquely Alive!, Activating Change, and Liberating Practices. You can either select a prayer by topic, or start with the first meditation and proceed in sequence, or choose a theme intuitively.

Read the invocation and then meditate. Let your imagination soar, hover, float, bask and ascend - ever higher, wider and deeper. Close by reading the blessing and allowing some time for releasing. Then reflect on the questions or comments on the opposite page.

You may find it helpful to stay with one theme for an entire week. Reflect on it every morning and review your day through its lens in the evening. Let the theme imbue and expand your awareness. Keep a journal to write down synchronicities, experiences and insights over the next several days. Invite this practice to help you see who you are, and tend, mend and befriend yourself. Relax any self-judgment and striving, and settle into your natural wisdom and authentic expression.

Each meditation fosters a sense of engagement with the forces of creativity, friendship and commitment. They exhort us to take personal responsibility and the initiative to let go and let life happen. Each application encourages us to accept our humanity and float our flaws and failures on a sea of self-observation, forgiveness, kindness, compassion and humor.

I'm so grateful to the Angel of Cluny Hill for encouraging me to write and speak up. Sharing these Sanctuaries completes a cycle for me and allows me to give back to the Findhorn Foundation some of the life-changing inspiration I received while living there. Additionally, if these meditations help you to navigate the changes in your life with curiosity, willingness and wholeheartedness, that's yet another gift they've given.

As you know, transformation has its own timetable. It cannot be hurried, but it can be cheered on. The way you treat yourself matters. The way you explore the contents of your own heart and mind makes a difference. The choices you make each day determine not only your next steps but also our collective future.

May these prayers strengthen your soul and support you in living a heartfelt, soul-infused life.

With many blessings,

Joy Drake
Asheville, 2015

Getting Started

Begin by closing your eyes.

Slow down, relax, soften and focus on your breathing.
Then in your mind's eye travel
to your inner sanctuary.

A place, real or imagined, where you feel at ease and at peace.
Your sanctuary might be a favorite chair in your home, a place of worship,
or a beautiful location in nature.

Imagine yourself sitting in this sacred space.

Rest in your sanctuary for a while receiving what it has to offer before moving on.

• For immediate self-reflection:

Review the prayer and blessing.
Then read the theme's application on the opposite page.
Note any initial realizations and take them into your day.

• To delve deeper:

Read the invocation out loud.
Meditate.
Then breathe out the blessing.
Stimulate further self-discovery by reflecting upon
and exploring the theme's application and questions.

New Beginnings

Inviting the Sacred into Everyday Life

Your life is a grand adventure.
Take risks.
Explore the unknown.
Journey forth into the great wide open
without pre-planned outcomes.

1: a whole new world

- invocation

>let us awaken to the gift of today
>and the splendid potential for creative service which it bears
>
>love is everywhere present
>everywhere available
>
>reach out
>
>trust that love will support you
>
>be sure of that
>be sure of yourself
>
>can you believe that a new world; its patterns, its forms, and its destiny rests within you?
>
>as you move
>move forward in certainty
>and stay open to the unexpected
>
>asking always
>what is the new pattern that is seeking emergence through me now?

. . . . (• meditation •) . . . .

- blessing

>from within this peaceful clearing, this space of light and openness
>may new patterns come to birth
>
>collectively now let our loving kindness shine forth
>
>embracing the hearts of all
>
>welcoming and blessing all life on earth

Inviting the Sacred . . .

1: a whole new world

We are the point where the rubber of our soul nature meets the road of our everyday lives. We are the tip of the divine pen: a kind of sacred-every-day alchemical change machine.

And here's the thing. Apparently divine pens like us were not meant to sit in joyous contemplation of our essential natures 24/7, but to do so within the blur of the breakfast-lunch-dinner routine, drive-work-play-errands-surprises flow of everyday busyness. Even more, our divine pen-ness is not only expected to notice new patterns but also change our old ones. Oh my, how can this possibly be done?

Well, I wish I could pass along a magical multipurpose mantra or password you could punch in or chant so that your way forward would be instantly apparent. Curiously one thing about uniqueness (you-niqueness) is that your you-ness really is different than mine or anyone else's. I can share my map, but you have to make your own journey and midwife your own creations.

Here's another thing. If you don't know what patterns need changing simply ask. Trust me on this. Depending on your willingness to see, your willingness to receive the answer, you will be given precisely what you need to get the job done - and then some.

What patterns have been gently tugging at the edge of your awareness?

What is one old pattern you can drop?

What new pattern can you add in and nurture?

As a divine pen what are you going to write today?

. . . . (• notes •) . . . .

2: engage with life

- invocation

      as we welcome this day
      let us become conscious of the brand new space
      available to us for enlightened thought and action

      today is a playground, a work department, a meeting place

      teeming with opportunities for us to love one another
      move beyond safe secure limits and contact the divine

      it's really very simple

      say yes to life's invitation to play
      then use every opportunity to engage your passion
      and give free rein to your co-creative flair

      keyword; engage . . .

. . . . (• meditation •) . . . .

- blessing

      we are all participants in the one life, bearers of the one light

      as we liberate our passion and allow our enthusiasm to flow out
      we nourish all life, all prospects, all possibilities

      as we take the opportunity now to engage with our passion
      we allow our dream of a heaven on earth to be realized
      right here and right now

2: engage with life

Say yes to life's invitation to play and engage your passion.
Make a commitment to let your mind run off-leash and give your creativity free rein.

Today does not have to be a copy of yesterday. Every moment brings a brand new canvas.
No matter how long you have done things a certain way, challenge yourself to change.

I know that moving out of a routine that you have been following for a while feels uncomfortable and risky but the rewards are really worth it.

Start small. Ruts are easy to spot. Change a habit that is insignificant. Walking around your yard in a different direction; spontaneously shifting the position of a chair, plant or papers can liberate your divine child who is unreservedly loving and excited about life. Suddenly life seems teaming with creative invitations in all directions.

Use every opportunity to engage afresh.
It's like getting a new rut-free lease on life.

Are you ready to play?

. . . . (• notes •) . . . .

3: first class of the day

- invocation

>we are all enrolled in a spiritual school
>
>this is the first class of the day
>it is directed by our spiritual elders
>and begins as we open our inner lesson books
>and inscribe a personal statement of intent
>
>beloved
>i am ready
>i am ready to assist in every way possible
>regardless of the changes I may have to make
>
>i am ready to move
>to step up in the light and receive your gifts, blessings and challenges
>and use them diligently to further our relationship
>to further my highest interests and the well being of my community
>
>my beloved soul
>i am willing to learn what is being taught here
>
>how may I serve today?

. . . . (• meditation •) . . . .

- blessing

>our schooling continues through the day
>and many other teachers will assist us
>
>as we emerge from this first classroom
>let us keep our lesson books and inner senses open
>as we watch our love, our understanding, and our gratitude merge
>and flow out into our planet on brilliant rays of light
>
>joyfully praising the divine in all
>
>and the perfect educational facilities here on earth

3: first class of the day

How often have you started a course or series of classes filled with enthusiasm and great dreams only to discover that it's a hard slog and the basics are boring.

Living life as a mystery school is, from one perspective, a hard slog. There's always more homework than anticipated. The curriculum requires more focus, time, energy, commitment - everything. It's a huge investment. Nothing is off limits. All is subject to change. Plus the pressure comes from within as the dynamic, irresistible motion of spirit meets the immoveable, resistant nature of matter.

The good news is that change is always possible and you, yes you, will graduate.

Remember it all depends on your point of view.
If you mention high pressure to meteorologists in winter they'll say,
"Ah, it's a wonderful thing."

. . . . (• notes •) . . . .

4: here is your present

- invocation

> life is a pilgrimage
> it is a flow through time eternal
>
> so relax into the journey
>
> let go
> offer no resistance
>
> trust the gentleness of the wind
> be at peace with the rain
> give yourself over to the currents of the river and drift with the ease of clouds
>
> for all these with you belong to the design of life
> they respond to the seasons
> respond with them
> it is your rightful heritage to do so
>
> allow what life is to manifest through you
> for above all life is action and change
> get into action, welcome change
>
> know that all actions once afoot end in one purpose
> recognize this, trust this, have faith in this and be a blessing in each of life's moments
>
> love life . . . . . you were meant to do nothing less
> see life . . . . . . it is evolving all around you
> respect life . . . it yearns to have your respect
>
> for life belongs to the design over which you and all humanity have dominion

> . . . . (• meditation •) . . . .

- blessing

> here is your present
> a season of earthly life
>
> inhabit your present
> live it at the height of your consciousness
> live it wholeheartedly
>
> choose the path of most allowing
> be a blessing
> let yourself be blessed
>
> offer your love to the universe unreservedly
> let it radiate from here now
> and embrace the hearts of all

Inviting the Sacred . . .

4: here is your present

What a luxury it is this season of vibrant earthly life;
this gift of nature and one another.

Relax into the wild exhilarating roller coaster ride
of inner softening, shifting and exploration.

Let go, squeal if you want to, but suspend all judgment and let life guide you.

. . . . (• notes •) . . . .

5: rhythms of the sacred

- invocation

    listen

    the rhythms of the sacred are strong and steady
    they are the rhythms of God's love and light and power

    we lift our being to this rhythm and know that it flows within us as well

    beloved
    i accept my divinity
    i accept responsibility

    breathe sweetly through me
    let me see with your vision
    let me love as your heart

    beloved
    i am available
    i am ready

    how best would you have me serve today?

. . . . (• meditation •) . . . .

- blessing

    the rhythms of the sacred move strongly and steadily within you

    you are splendidly human
    you are gorgeously divine

    together let us be God-centered and human-hearted
    and bring the best of both worlds to all we do today

    that all we meet will benefit from our presence
    that this world may be truly blessed

5: rhythms of the sacred

in you the mystical and practical
merge

through you these two worlds express

and the soul's divine rhythm

arises as a strong, steady beat
propelling you where you need to be

dah-dum -- dah-dum -- dah-dum

May my feet move in synch with my soul's tempo.

. . . . (• notes •) . . . .

6: stay open

- invocation

> become aware of the presence of the divine
> in you
> in everything
>
> allow yourself to open
> open fully to that presence
>
> as you relate to people
> as you experience the world
> allow yourself to open even more
> become aware of the presence of the divine
> in each moment and in every circumstance
>
> recognize our common divinity
> our common purpose
> allow yourself to open to this
>
> open to life and stay open to others
> open to listen and stay open to hear
> open to love and stay open to change
>
> simply allow yourself to open
> and
> stay open . . . stay open

. . . . (• meditation •) . . . .

- blessing

> openness is the key that frees us from bondage to old patterns
>
> openness to let life in
> willingness to live life out
>
> and in the midst of very big things
> in the midst of very small things
> pause and open to the presence within
> remember who you are, what you are doing, why you are doing it
>
> and let our openness to life, to ourselves, and to each other spread out
> until there is no part of our world that is not filled with an awareness and radiance
> of the presence and blessings of the divine
>
> until there is no part of our world that is not filled with awareness and gratitude
> for a peaceful heart and loving earth

6: stay open

With hair-trigger sensitivity we can close down without even knowing it, without realizing it's happened. The slightest thing can push us into separateness and disconnect us from God, from oneself and others. All of a sudden we feel isolated and all we can hear is the chattering of our own mind worries.

This is why frequent pauses, naps, deep breathing and intentional resting are so useful; times to go easy, be soft and gentle and let go into the light of love.

A few conscious, generous breaths can effortlessly reconnect you to divine presence and you can breathe new life into the moment. Just as suddenly it's easy to open up and you're in the flow again.

One life potent and indivisible.
One divine heart connected to all hearts.

Simply take several slow, deep, opening breaths - in and out, and in and out ...

Slow down.
Soften.

Stay open to the vast healing presence of love.

. . . . (• notes •) . . . .

7: step out

• invocation

    become aware of your location

    you are right on the line

    choose now to cross over
    to rid yourself of defenses, presumptions, facades
    and express who you truly are

    step out without hesitation
    beyond your dreams
    beyond your drama
    and into the joy of life

    step into the unknown, into the new
    and let your love flow freely

    life is meant to be enjoyed
    not coped with or moved through
    open up and release the old you
    let it go

    let your integrity guide you and let the new emerge

    let the new you emerge

    . . . . (• meditation •) . . . .

• blessing

    become aware of your location
    and step fully into the now

    the promised land is here
    the promised time is now
    born of our unity and our love

    let the power of this affirmation flow forth

    see it sweep across the earth as a golden light
    awakening
    revitalizing
    blessing all
    welcoming the new day

    let every soul rejoice as the light of heaven becomes one with earth

Inviting the Sacred . . .

7: step out

Become aware of your location.

- *Where in yourself are you standing?*

- *Are you standing on the edge of the known world hovering a few feet from your past?*

- *Is your world divided into neatly labeled compartments in which you have got it all sorted and know how things work?*

- *Are you in the same place as you were yesterday and last week?*

At some point I think we each need to give up control and jump beyond our lines, our divisions, our dreams, and our dramas and into the truth of life. It takes great courage to let go. To do so is to step out of one's personal history and stand alone in the secret of a new and totally unique moment.

Go on!

Give it a go right now.

Put all your energy into this moment and step fully into the new!

relax . . . breathe

watch and welcome

. . . . (• notes •) . . . .

8: strengthen your commitment

• invocation

> how far does your commitment extend?
> where do you draw the line in reaching out to others?
>
> becoming aware that you draw lines is the first step
> now we are asked to step over our lines and follow through
>
> for whatever is in front of you is yours to complete
> seize the opportunity and get started
> stay with it and follow through to completion
>
> this is spiritual dependability
> the universal key that opens all doors
>
> as you open doors for others today
> you will discover more of yourself
> and step over the threshold into a new and greater reality

. . . . (• meditation •) . . . .

• blessing

> we are all learning not to draw lines
>
> no lines between you and divinity
> no lines between you and me
>
> being here involves not only eloquent speeches
> but the intentional living of elegant lives
>
> being here involves deliberately, skillfully and reliably choosing to step beyond our lines
>
> let us step forward now
> strengthening our commitment
> and extending our love, light, wisdom and purpose outward from this center
> so that the earth may most purely experience the spirit of the God moving upon it today

Inviting the Sacred . . .

8: strengthen your commitment

Personally, socially, culturally and organizationally we all have boundaries.
They are a natural, organic way to distinguish this from that.
But rigid boundaries can become barriers and self-managing prisons.

Whatever your past, nothing can imprison your spirit now.

Whatever your circumstances you can find a way to mentally and emotionally
erase non-serving barriers and let your love, light and joi-de-vivre flow freely.

Strengthen your commitment to step beyond your lines and dramas today.
Step into the truth and joy of life.

Voice your desire, set your intention and soften your edges.

Then step forward

and give it all you've got!

. . . . (• notes •) . . . .

9: we are infinite beings

- invocation

    we are infinite beings discovering our finiteness

    we cannot be limited
    we cannot be separated from the divine
    for infinity reaches to all corners of the material world with ease

    creating our spiritual path means treading carefully on this earthly one
    for matters of seeming insignificance on this plane
    often hold the potential for greatest expansion

    we are infinite beings discovering our finiteness

    if I can keep my bathroom floor clean consistently
    then I'll know I'm really evolving

. . . . (• meditation •) . . . .

- blessing

    the new world is all around us if it is within us
    guiding and teaching us with infinite love and patience
    how to create a joyful, peaceful and loving world

    we appreciate the splendor of the divine presence that partners with us

    and we visualize our group as a radiant chalice in which all energies unite in light
    to bless our beloved earth

    we are moving
    we are evolving

    let today demonstrate and affirm our progress

9: we are infinite beings

How consistently do you walk your talk?

There is little point in having a glorious inner life if your outer everyday life is in a shambles.

Look around your house and car.

Scan your primary relationships.

Reassess your work and social life.

These areas directly reflect the extent to which you are transporting infinity into this time space continuum and embodying your highest intentions.

Is each area uncluttered, loving, exciting, adventurous, unrestricted and growing?

If you find a gap or glitch breathe love into it and then take action.

Jettison outdated excess baggage.
You know where to start.

Just do one thing.

. . . . (• notes •   ) . . . .

Uniquely Alive!

Welcoming the Sacred into Everyday Life

Add your unique ingredients to the mix.
Be real.
Express yourself.
Uncloak your originality
and manifest your pure potential.

10: are you living a spiritual life?

• invocation

what's involved in living a spiritual life?

spirit is at home all over the place
spirit animal
spirit vegetable
spirit mineral
spirit vertical, horizontal, spherical, conical, and fractal
solid spirit liquid spirit vapor spirit

spirit moving in waves
merging ~ emerging ~~ merging ~ emerging
so you can't tell one state from the other
spirit one day from form the next
mind one minute from heart the next

understand you are spirit
you are a free spirit
you chose this lifetime, this personality
now you are here, affirm your choice in every moment
live enormously
live lightly

are you living a spiritual life?
are you moving?
are you emerging?
are you at home all over the place?
entirely present in any situation?

if you can do it . . . . . . it is done

. . . . (• meditation •) . . . .

• blessing

into this day we allow the light of spirit to guide us
we open our hearts to the power of love
and open our minds to the new and unexpected

we deepen our commitment and willingness to serve
and expand the realm of spirit on earth

reaffirm your personal commitment now
letting it be so complete and entire
that spirit flows through you unimpeded and out into the world

now and throughout this day

Welcoming the Sacred . . .

10: are you living a spiritual life?

Am I living a spiritual life? At first glance the answer seems kind of obvious.
Well of course I'm living a spiritual life, how could I not?

Plus being a free spirit sounds like lots of fun.

♪ ♩ ♪ ♫ Zip - Ah - De - Doo - Dah, Zip - Ah - Dee - A ♪ ♩ ♪ ♫

Appraise honestly how consciously and joyfully you are living your life.

Take this moment to celebrate your willingness to let spirit flow through you unimpeded into your world today.

Then renew your commitment to relax and live the life you love; satisfied with where you are and eager for more.

. . . . (• notes •) . . . .

11: boldly go

• invocation

    give yourself fully to the process of creation

    you are here to learn how to do just this
    and it is necessary for you to be courageous
    to develop clear-sightedness
    and have confidence in your ability to be

    for it is at such moments that you can face yourself honestly
    freed from illusions and misconceptions

    such experiences are not for the timid

    it is time to come out of the shadows and step into the light
    it is time to accept fully the splendor of who you are
    and the work you have come to do

    this is the life to do it in
    now is the time to do it

    all the other kingdoms are here to support your emergence
    let go and allow yourself to be supported

    come out and own up to life
    be bold
    let life in
    let the contact be made

. . . . (• meditation •) . . . .

• blessing

    give yourself fully to the process of creation

    accept your resources

    you are beloved
    you belong to the family of life
    you have been given the kingdom and space to create in it

    dare to use it
    your response will be perfect

    just try it
    let divine love, light and peace stream through you
    opening the way for greater blessings and greater goodness to boldly manifest
    on our beautiful planet earth

11: boldly go

Are you willing to step out of the shadows?

What are you passionate about? What excites you? What gives you joy?

Where in your life do you need to step forward?

If you were completely free where would you boldly go today?

live your life to the fullest
let the contact be made

be bold

make it so!

. . . . (• notes •) . . . .

12: illuminating your way

• invocation

> life force
> the power of spirit to manifest
> is placing us all on the spot
>
> it is the same one
> the focal point of emergence into the new
>
> we have pushed open the gateway
> now we find ourselves living in an unknown reality
> the one certainty being that there is no going back
>
> we are here now
>
> everything is just the same and totally different
> we are standing on terra firma but the ground feels unfamiliar, shifting
> the good old ways and comfortable routine days are over
>
> replaced by a sense of divine humor
> that challenges us to be inventive, open and honest
>
> replaced by a high adventure
> whose outcome depends on our complete acceptance of our shared divinity
> upon our willingness to aspire to and achieve the highest
>
> the comfortable old days are over and the only way on is through
> know that only the lantern of your inner spirit can guide your way on
> let it shine
> let it show you your way
>
> if you ask sincerely you will be shown

. . . . (• meditation •) . . . .

• blessing

> may the transformative power of our souls
> illuminate our many ways
> that we may each see the truth and trust it enough to act from it consistently
>
> let the lantern of each spirit here shine forth
> let us see this tremendous downpouring of infinite love streaming outwards
>
> feel it flowing through us embracing the hearts of all
> heralding new life . . . new ways . . . new days
>
> uplifting all into the light of new possibilities

12: illuminating your way

Remember that your partnership with spirit is a win-win arrangement.

However dark your outlook or surroundings appear to be, trust the lantern of your inner spirit to illuminate your way, reinforce your desire to keep moving, and guide you on your path.

Let your soul-light shine.

Let it show you your way.

If you ask sincerely you will be shown – so ask!

Where do you need the light to shine today?

. . . . (• notes •) . . . .

13: joy of living

• invocation

    as individuals we hold a beautiful vision

    coming together we find the strength to live that dream and make it a reality
    for as long as we are here we have a job to do
    and a purpose to fulfill
    and that means dealing with the circumstances around us

    dealing with the circumstances around us the very best that we can
    as honestly, openly, clearly, and lovingly as we can

    awakened to the fact that everything that happens to us is perfect
    relates directly to who we are and is playing its role in fulfilling our destiny

    asking always
    what can I learn from this?
    how will it strengthen me?

    we are being strengthened
    we are growing
    we are en-joying
    we are living life to the fullest

    this is the real work and we are doing it perfectly

    on purpose

    together

. . . . (• meditation •) . . . .

• blessing

    our destiny is unimaginably high

    hold fast to your vision
    let yourself open wide to embrace it

    for to that extent is love and light and the joy of living released into the world

13: joy of living

Dealing with the circumstances around us sounds so simple but when a situation is not to our liking we tend to fuss, (this isn't what I want), whine, (there must be some mistake), and moan and groan. We also tend to run in the other direction, which adds even more stress.

How deep is the contrast between where you are and where you want to be?

Enjoying here when we'd prefer to be over there, that's what it's all about.
Acceptance is like a soothing balm that reduces emotional wrinkles and moisturizes trust.

Take a few moments to pause. Slow down.
Remember that you have a direct, no-waiting pipeline to the wisdom of your soul.

Open the valve, make the connection and smile.

Lay down your petulance and offer your availability and innocence instead.

Ask your questions and say yes to everything that arises.

. . . . (• notes •) . . . .

14: let go

• invocation

>we are each involved
>in the most intimate, penetrating, revealing relationship
>
>constantly exposing us
>drawing us up
>drawing us closer
>to one another, to the divine
>
>we are asked to let the highest emerge and are given the vision to see clearly
>any attachments or dependencies that might be getting in the way
>and offered the opportunity to release them and unclutter our lives
>
>it means letting go and moving with new impulses
>experiencing new ways of being ourselves
>new ways of knowing each other
>
>now there is the possibility to understand
>our humanity through our divinity
>our divinity through our humanity
>our wholeness through our willingness and openness
>
>may receptivity to the new fill this group
>may we let go and allow the highest to emerge

. . . . (• meditation •) . . . .

• blessing

>as we let go we see ourselves with new eyes
>we see one another with renewed appreciation
>and we can approach the world with clearsight, compassion and ease
>
>let these blessings flow out now to those we know and love
>and further to bless and cover the whole world
>with compassion . . . clearsight . . . and ease
>
>visualize humanity
>at home
>on earth
>
>held in the peace, poise and prosperity of this divine moment

14: let go

- *Do you hold a family member in a special set of expectations?*

- *Do you hold any of your co-workers or friends in a particular set of expectations?*

- *What do you expect of yourself?*

- *What do you expect of the world?*

We have been trained by experts to spot what is wrong. We can notice what is out of kilter at a thousand paces and talk (endlessly) about what hurts, what rubs us up the wrong way, and how unfairly and unbearably our boat is being rocked.

Now we are asked to look for what is right with the world, what is working in our lives and to talk (endlessly) about that.

Imagine that for the next 24 hours you do just that. You speak only about what feels good, about what you are grateful for, who you appreciate, how well things are going; the good stuff. Put your attention on experiences you want to generate and notice what you notice.

If you slip up, simply refocus and start over.

When you get to 24 hours give yourself a gold star, a healthy treat, and begin again.

. . . . (• notes •) . . . .

15: precision flying

• invocation

>lift yourself out of ignorance
>step outside and greet life
>there is no one else to do it
>
>life is contagious
>catch it
>
>here are some guidelines
>take courage
>pay attention
>have fun and trust
>
>your wings will respond automatically, perfectly, always
>
>understand
>you are spirit
>you are a free spirit
>you may go in any direction you choose
>
>you chose this life, this personality
>now you are here affirm your choice in every moment
>
>live impeccably
>move beyond your boundaries
>experience precision flying
>
>live expansively . . . purposefully . . . joyfully
>if you can do it . . . it is done

. . . . (• meditation •) . . . .

• blessing

>we are here to make contact with the world
>
>we are here to spread our wings
>and, as we do so, the golden light of spirit born of our unity and love
>flows freely forth encircling the earth
>blessing all
>
>it is the season of rebirth
>let every soul rejoice as light descends on earth

15: precision flying

Let love adjust your wing tilt.
Let life provide the wind drafts you need when you need them.

Stay awake, aware and appreciative of the friends who are flying shoulder to shoulder alongside you. Feel the feathering of your combined presence.

Feel the high adventure of adapting to a series of unplanned, precise, emerging moments.

Feel the rush.

. . . . (• notes •) . . . .

16: release the old

- invocation

      within this room
      within each of us
      is a tremendous power

      it is the presence of spirit
      claiming this center
      claiming each of us
      calling us to follow up on our commitments to divine purpose

      it is attachments that bind us to the old
      the routines, the patterns of behavior
      the pieces of us that have become inflexible and resistant
      when we meet a new situation all of us can respond to it
      except our attachments

      now we are asked to free up and unclutter our lives
      it means letting go of controls, demands and convenient ways
      and intentionally harnessing our lives to divine purposes

      it means releasing attachments
      finding new ways of being
      Inviting new ways of seeing
      seeking new ways of serving

      but - didn't you say you wanted freedom?

      . . . . (• meditation •) . . . .

- blessing

      visualize yourself radiant, free and whole

      loving yourself
      loving those around you
      acting with excellence, surety and balance

      this is an important day for each of us
      a day of actualizing our inner selves
      and creating supportive connections with the world

      in doing this work together
      we release radiations of tremendous healing power
      that flow outwards bathing our planet in the beauty and light of a new consciousness
      and, like soft warm rain, blessing and nourishing all life on earth

Welcoming the Sacred . . .

16: release the old

If you've said for years that all you wanted was freedom but did little about it - life, always willing to help out, might provide the momentum you need to set yourself free.

Perhaps you lose your job, a primary relationship is uncoupled, your body gets sick, etc. Nothing is off-limits. Crises grab our attention and propel us into the rinse cycle of life so we can let go of all that is outmoded and do what it was we have been avoiding.

Life moves us from aspiration, prayer and intention into swim, fly or deep rest mode.

Of course you could shut down indefinitely and become embittered, resentful and crustacean-like, but I recommend clambering through any open doorway into your heart and residing there in the tenderness, warmth and freedom of love's grace for a while.

Not just once a day or even once an hour, but over and over, again and again until trusting feels natural and loving kindness and compassion is your only response to everything.

. . . . (• notes •) . . . .

17: unifying presence

• invocation

      there is a presence here
      a divine presence
      feel it now
      a holy spirit that streams through the galaxy
      and draws the universe together
      and draws us together
      in this sacred spot

      a presence
      the source of our beings
      who knows us intimately
      who is who we are
      and who loves us unconditionally

      turn within and feel the radiance and love of this presence within you
      let your thoughts flow towards this source of inner light
      open to it
      and merge with it
      willingly

      let go of the known, safe and familiar
      yield to the divine power within
      and let it guide you into new life and an experience of unity

. . . . (• meditation •) . . . .

• blessing

      this is an important day for each of us
      a day of being in perfect harmony with divine will
      and accepting personal responsibility for all we experience

      let us welcome this new day
      and recognize the teachers and lessons
      the answers and opportunities it offers us for stillness, for service and change

      sense now a merging of our individual suns
      as our anticipation shines out from here on rays of light
      that carry affirmations of warmth, expectancy and vitality

      we bathe the earth with the unifying presence of the divine
      one presence here . . . now . . .

17: unifying presence

Here's the really wonderful news. You were born with the capacity to tap into, commune with, and navigate fields of infinite change, expansion and healing. How neat is this?

You can pause, postpone, or interrupt your usual way of perceiving a situation. You can let go of the known, safe and familiar and try something different. You can be adventurous. You can shake things up. Instead of a yes/no attitude to life, you can offer more yesses and evolve a refreshing friendship with yourself and with the divine.

Co-creation begins when you say yes - unreservedly. This is the work now. The tide is coming in, powerfully and rapidly, and movement is unavoidable for us. We are to come alive by saying yes to what is, yes to love, light, truth, joys, sorrows, yes to our experience, yes to one another, yes to life.

Yes. Yes. Yes. Yes. Yes. Yes. Yes . . . and moreover I yield.

Only you can show us how wonderful life is when you bring a unifying presence wherever you go, and let the new spring forth in offices, airports, supermarkets, waiting rooms and other sacred temples of learning. Only you.

. . . . (• notes •) . . . .

18: unwrapping

• invocation

>we are each a gift to the other
>no need to cover up
>
>let go of your old trappings
>
>plain and fancy wrappings are expensive, worthless, and useless
>because there's no need to hide
>
>let the barriers fall away
>become visible
>become yourself
>
>as barely
>as essentially
>as wholly as you are
>
>we are here to give ourselves completely in service
>so let us reach out
>open up
>surrender
>and know the gifts of God within

. . . . (• meditation •) . . . .

• blessing

>we are changing
>
>sometimes it seems very slow
>sometimes very sudden
>but we are changing and as we do so the world changes
>
>this is the work
>
>we have opened this day by opening ourselves
>let us maintain this visibility as we release into the world
>the light of our understanding and the wisdom of our love
>
>see and feel these gifts radiating from this sanctuary now
>purifying and revitalizing the planet and all the beings who share our home

18: unwrapping

• Do you feel as if your life is spinning out of control?

• Do you feel as if you are coming undone?

• Is life as you know it unraveling?

Could it be that the emerging divine impulse is unwrapping you so that you can live unencumbered by old cover-ups you've being praying to discard for so long?

Perhaps your deep opinion of yourself is being reconstructed and, as you unpeel your bubble wrap with compassion, you can shift to a new perception of you. When you surrender and allow love and gratitude in the midst of the dismantling, dramas fall away and dissolve, and the best way to think about what's next is revealed.

This is the way you are molting to your core.

Uncloak your beauty . . . unwrap the gift of you.

• What family wrapping paper did you grow up with that you are now ready to discard?

. . . . (• notes •) . . . .

Activating Change

Appreciating the Sacred in Everyday Life

Change happens when you take responsibility for your
awareness and apply it to your everyday life
small moment by small moment.

19: affirmations of love

- invocation

  where is love?

  where is love?

. . . . (• meditation •) . . . .

- blessing

  love is the heartbeat of the galaxy
  connecting us to the pulse of the universe
  carrying us beyond the stars

  and love is a seed planted within every human heart
  will you leave it a seed or bring it forth to blossom in the garden of your life?

  open your heart

  visualize yourself anchoring the highest vibration of love

  love, unconditional and infinite, flowing freely
  through every relationship and each situation that you are involved in today

  and as a group let us imagine that we are standing at the center of the earth
  letting our love flow out to stir and quicken the seeds within the hearts of humanity
  creating earth a radiant garden of perfect love and peace

  we affirm our love

  we affirm our love

19: affirmations of love

So where is love?

Love is wherever you imagine it, dream it and look for it to be - inside and out.

First open your heart, then you'll spot love everywhere, you'll feel love coming to life through you . . . right here and right now.

Can you translate this knowing into all your relationships? (I love you)

Especially your relationship with yourself? (I love you - I love you)

Relocate yourself in a universe where there is only love.
Let it bless all the ages and stages of your journey. Then wherever you look, inside and out, there love is beaming "I love you" right back at you.

Feel grateful for all that has allowed you to be alive at this moment and for the opportunity to witness what love can do.

Next question?

. . . . (• notes •) . . . .

20: dare to love

- invocation

  how can you assist planetary transformation?

  by welcoming personal changes
  by willingly taking responsibility for your life

  what you're putting in
  what you're putting out

  how can you assist planetary transformation?

  by simply being yourself

  standing in power
  resting in love
  living in joy

  and letting the natural radiance of your soul's light illuminate your way

  . . . . (• meditation •) . . . .

- blessing

  how can we assist planetary transformation?

  by daring to love
  daring to imagine
  daring to achieve the very highest

  a joyful vision of earth
  slowly moving in soft golden light
  supporting the garden of our humanity and the evolution of all lives

  let us hold this vision clearly before us now and throughout today
  letting the radiance of our souls
  light our way on

  inspiring each other
  uplifting all

Appreciating the Sacred . . .

20: dare to love

Planetary transformation sounds huge and complex but it's really very simple.

What are you putting in?

What are you putting out?

What quality of presence would you like to cultivate and emanate?

Dare to imagine - dare to love - begin with yourself . . .

Your soul is waiting in the wings to help you. Simply ask the radiance of your soul's light to illuminate your next steps then pay attention to the highlighted choices that show up.

. . . . (• notes •) . . . .

21: it's up to you

• invocation

    appreciate your divine attributes

    you are gifted with the courage to give from your heart always
    you are gathered here now to birth the new in love

    trust your responses and act on them
    let life serve you
    remind you of what you are doing

    love one another
    listen to one another
    take time to communicate
    to create together

    approach life openly
    risk all you have attained so far to rely on the creative process
    leave room for alternatives not yet dreamed of
    do all that has to be done to let the inherent flow be fully available

    trust yourself
    trust one another

    the way to learn how
    is to simply do it

    it's up to you
    it's all up to you

. . . . (• meditation •) . . . .

• blessing

    behold the kingdom of heaven is here now
    boundless and free

    its power is within each of us
    the power of knowing, of giving, of trusting, of allowing

    use your power wisely that together we may be the living light
    that gives new life to the sacred

    now let our light shine forth
    awakening humanity to the radiant beauty of their own souls
    and the truth of our relationship to the divine

                                              Appreciating the Sacred . . .

21: it's up to you

Here's the thing about learning to trust yourself. You are human and therefore not infallible. So don't keep retracing your steps along this pathway of thought.

Learning to trust yourself involves taking risks especially in your relationships. This requires being sensitive to the moment and what the moment is calling for, like being willing to share how you feel. It may also involve shifting the way you view others and how you think others view you. Risks incur the element of uncertainty and risks can liberate great power and change the course of history - your history.

Don't get up from reading this until you've touched love - until you feel embraced and embracing, supported and supporting, until you feel infused with love. Consciously breathe into and through your open heart. Sit for a while soaking in and resting in its loving, healing essence.

Trust is at the heart of all that is unfolding. Rest, drive, cook and chat today from the trust in your heart. Then wherever you are becomes a sanctuary.

How will you invest your trust today?

. . . . (• notes •) . . . .

22: our pledge to spirit

• invocation

>our pledge to spirit is total
>it permeates and directs every moment of every day
>it is our most intimate, penetrating and exacting relationship
>
>our contract is service to the whole
>our agreement - to love
>our commitment - to love one another consistently and reliably
>here on earth
>
>so when we meet
>whenever, wherever that happens
>we are charged with the responsibility
>to be fully present to one another
>and ensure that the connection with spirit
>the connection with love, is made real in human expression
>
>spirit is claiming this center
>spirit is claiming each one of us
>open up
>let go and allow love to move through more of you
>
>to touch more of us

. . . . (• meditation •) . . . .

• blessing

>we are floating on the waters of spirit
>it is the fluid of love that bathes our individual landforms
>and links the continent of our humanity
>
>as we renew our pledge to spirit
>let us deepen our highest connections with one another
>
>let our love and light flow outwards from this sanctuary
>
>see it sweep across the earth
>awakening
>refreshing
>cleansing
>healing
>
>welcoming the new day
>strengthening and revitalizing the web of interlacing spiritual light

Appreciating the Sacred . . .

22: our pledge to spirit

Making a pledge to spirit is a promise to love.
It's about connecting with your spirit daily.
It's about living your purpose from your heart and not letting yourself down.

Take at least five minutes in each busy day to sit in silence.

Sit with yourself stripped bare, honoring your pledge and simply being.

Let yourself be embraced, soothed, nurtured and blessed by life's healing salve - love.
Let it bathe your individual landform with unsurpassable shining glory.

- *What really matters?*

- *What's your highest priority?*

- *What comes first?*

Keep expanding your capacity to love and be loved.

. . . . (• notes •) . . . .

23: paradise now

- invocation

> paradise

> just imagine there is paradise in and around you right now
> just as you are
> and to be there you don't even have to make a move

> simply be open to the perfection of all that is

> allow your love to be constant
> and experience life without mental resistance

> once you accept an identity of wholeness
> you accept that all is contained within you
> and you begin to incorporate the whole

> act from this space
> stay open to all life offers
> and make a total commitment to loving yourself
> and loving others unreservedly

. . . . (• meditation •) . . . .

- blessing

> we are here to become spiritually dependable
> and all the angels in heaven and on earth are here to assist us

> just imagine . . . infinite energy . . . life abundant
> you are wealthy beyond measure

> use your resources
> have confidence in your connectedness
> have confidence in your wholeness
> and as we travel together let joy be our compass

> let us consciously allow our brightness and joy to shine forth
> to bless, lighten and enliven our world

> free-flowing . . . lush . . . whole
> our paradise now

23: paradise now

Paradise is defined as any place or conditions that fulfill all one's desires or aspirations.

What will it take for you to allow your current environment and circumstances to be a bit more paradisiacal, heavenly, free-flowing, healed, whole - perfect in its imperfections.

What can you do in this moment to make where you are paradise?

. . . . (• notes •) . . . .

24: soaking in grace

• invocation

>you are a landing pad for grace
>a vortex of immeasurable power

>you are here on purpose

>you are here to embody love and let spirit move through you, as you
>you are here to let your soul stand revealed
>you are here to live authentically, creatively, joyfully

>as an expression of grace
>you fully represent all that is

. . . . (• meditation •) . . . .

• blessing
you are an anchor for grace

you are here to manifest love and let spirit fill every corner of your life
you are here to express truth and give voice to your soul
you are here to join in the dance of life

together we form a vibrant chalice filled to overflowing with divine blessings

let us hold back none of our gifts and talents
rather let our love be constant and our light so shine
that it radiates from this circle as an unquenchable wave of goodness
washing the world with tenderness, adaptability and prosperity

soaking the world in grace

24: soaking in grace

Remember that you're part of a living chalice of grace whether you are in a chalice-like setting or not. Take time every day, however briefly, to rest in this identity.

Imagine you are in a soak cycle in the washing machine of life. You are all washed up. So let yourself go limp and soak up the grace of the divine. Absorb and assimilate the grace and feel your whole system being professionally rinsed; spiritually unclogged, mentally upgraded, emotionally boosted, physically healed and deeply transformed.

No sooner thought than done.

Take a few moments at work, when you get in your car, before you eat, check your email, or pick up the phone to take a full breath and remember you are soaking in grace.

Affirm
I am an anchor for grace.
I am soaking the world in grace.

Invite your divine nature to deeply penetrate, permeate and infiltrate every particle of your body, mind and heart. Allow the graceful presence of who you are to come through.

Ask yourself, where does grace want to come into my life today?

Imagine yourself as grace in motion.

. . . . (• notes •) . . . .

25: soul sight

• invocation

behold the world with soul sight

create your own realm of peace and love
let wise action and joyous dedication be your rule

let the purposes of the divine direct and guide you
quieting the battles and clearing the ground of inner conflicts
letting peace and fulfillment reign
allowing the song of your joyful spirit to fill the air

for as you gratefully and creatively accept all the world presents you with
you claim, with power and authority, your spiritual leadership
and enable humanity to emerge into the light and presence of reunion with the divine

. . . . (• meditation •   ) . . . .

• blessing

reach upwards and open outwards

we are together now to receive the highest blessings
that are appropriate to this day

may they awaken our intuition
our creative imagination
our highest mental capacities
and our collective love

that through the steadfastness of our relationships
the purity of our speech and the clarity of our activities
we may inspire one another
and behold the world with soul sight

in so doing we become a blessing for the world
and we allow the plan of love and light to unfold in grace

we behold the world with soul sight

25: soul sight

Seeing yourself, others and the world with soul sight means taking off your customized blinders, your personality filters, and letting go of the desire for things to go a certain way.

It means strengthening and toning your inner-sight muscles of compassionate attention and adaptability so you can widen or shrink your perspective and see the soul's panorama in the greatest and the tiniest with clarity, objectivity and a soaring, grateful heart.

Commit to working your soul-sight muscles today
and having a good time doing it.

Clear seeing with a lot of heart.

. . . . (• notes •) . . . .

26: spring cleaning

- invocation

  the heart is open

  be responsive to the thoughts of your heart
  to the divine you whose presence blesses all your activities
  all your considerations
  all your actions

  and let us join in agreement
  we are one

  in this agreement is power
  and with this power the work gets done
  as each of us consciously allows spirit to move into us and through us
  welcoming and initiating change

  and here we are this morning
  radiant
  expressive
  alive

  here and in the eternal now

. . . . (• meditation •) . . . .

- blessing

  we are learning to interact with the world

  we start from here
  from where we are
  and clean up all the rooms in our house

  we open all the doors and windows
  upstairs and downstairs
  and let in fresh sweet spring air

  we make our whole house a fitting dwelling place for the divine

  and as we open ourselves to the blessings of spirit
  our collective soul star shines clearly and brightly
  allowing love and light and wisdom to pass cleanly through us and out into the world

26: spring cleaning

We are awakening to a new season both personally and collectively.

The world is changing rapidly.
To keep pace we need to open all the love-windows and let in fresh, sweet air.

It's time to recalibrate and replenish our reserves.

Do whatever's needed to boost your vitality.

. . . . (• notes •) . . . .

27: warriorship 101

- invocation

  we are here to manifest love

  the days of viewing our lives as a glorified tickertape parade
  raining a random selection of blessings and curses
  dispensed by some vast almighty hand
  are clearly over - over to us

  a highly potent impulse is coming through
  and, as the outmoded parts of ourselves are stripped away
  we can experience life wholly instead of partially

  we can draw upon our inner strengths and develop clear-sightedness
  we can make conscious choices and be of service

  all we have to do is not shut anything out
  all we have to do is stay open and listen

  . . . . (• meditation •) . . . .

- blessing

  planetary restoration is a risky business
  it involves climbing up very high scaffolding and maintaining balance
  while drawing love for all down onto this earthly plane

  it takes courage, balance and a clear focus of intent
  and the reality is that we are doing it
  we are stepping into life unreservedly, lovingly, and joyously

  and every step we take today contributes directly and substantially
  to the world's aliveness
  the world's peace
  the world's joy

  let us affirm now, by taking a group step, our dedication to the divine
  and our total commitment to one another and the work we are doing together

  now starts the day
  joy in plenty to the world

27: warriorship 101

Planetary transformation sounds grand but it's really very simple and down to earth in the small tasks of everyday life. It's time to bring our lofty realizations and radiant goodness down to infuse the breakfast-lunch-dinner routine with creative possibilities and excellence, but how?

We need to see people applying loving kindness, courage and steadfastness in their lives, freeing themselves from self-made prisons, appreciating the beauty in themselves and the world, and offering their gifts and services without expectations.

Those who know must act unhesitatingly, making friends with life, and making light work of the perils and illusions of this world. Just imagine all the inner warriors, ALL of us getting up, leaving our doubts behind, picking up our power, purpose and passion and striding into loving action.

Are you ready and willing to let YOUR light shine, to express your joy fully,
to share your love without holding back?

Why wait any longer? If not you - then who?

There's just us here now.

Liberating Practices

Deepening the Sacred in Everyday Life

Your thoughts create.
Your actions matter.
Your presence changes everything.
Align with your essence.
Know your place, stand up fully in yourself,
and greet each moment afresh.

28: all our meetings

- invocation

> allow yourself to open
> to touch the essence of who you are
>
> love is the key
>
> as we come together
> let us experience fully the wonder of being together
> just as we really are
> just us as we are right now
>
> loving one another
> in touch
> whole
>
> knowing who we are
> clearly
> and fully
> we meet
>
> in the presence of one another
> in the presence of the divine

. . . . (• meditation •) . . . .

- blessing

> when we meet again
> in the kitchen
> the garden
> the lounge
>
> in the dining room
> the corridors
> or the bedrooms
>
> on the road
> or in the shop
>
> in all our meetings
> in any place
> let us remember who we are and what we are doing
> and make this essential contact of love with each other
>
> allowing the outcome of all our meetings
> to be released as a flow of light and love and joy
> augmenting the power and reality of spirit on earth

Deepening the Sacred . . .

28: all our meetings

It's all too easy to get caught up in busyness and take love for granted – to focus on completing the tasks on our to-do list, or get lost in the intricacies of our process and see only the drawbacks, flaws and incompleteness.

You see what you look for.
So look for things that you like, look for quirks you love, and cherish the ones that you find.

It's a discipline to look for the positive but it changes everything.

Make a practice to pause briefly between the segments of your day. Move your focus to your heart and listen. Try it before, during and at the end of every meeting. The essence of who you are is very available so contact with it, even momentarily, is deeply refreshing. Then, when you meet people, look for things that rub you the right way and notice the things about them that delight you.

Appreciation keeps your heart healthy and your emotional windscreen clear.

Start right now!

. . . . (• notes •) . . . .

29: filled with gratitude

• invocation

> in the peace and quiet at the end of this day
> let us be filled with gratitude for the life we are living

> what have we said and done today?

> what have we created in the universe today?

> as we review the day's events
> let us recognize ourselves and the patterns of our interactions
> from a point of clear perception and kindest regard

> can we take today and all that we have filled it with and offer it?

> owning the moments of clarity, definition, and pronouncement
> and owning the moments of fuzziness, hesitation, and doubt
> for the totality of who we are rests in none of these moments
> but flows through them all

> let us acknowledge the uniqueness of our journey and be filled with gratitude
> for all we have given today

> for all we have been given

. . . . (• meditation •) . . . .

• blessing

> now rests the day

> and we also rest
> filled with gratitude for the deep and profound love available to us at this time
> which we now share with our world

29: filled with gratitude

Gratitude nurtures the soul and completes the cycle.

Allow each day to be a broader celebration of gratitude than the day before.
Find new ways to appreciate yourself, others, and life's rich patterns. Say thank you like you mean it, like you wish it, like your fairy godmother just sprinkled you with gratitude dust.

Fill your heart with the feeling of gratitude. Let it flood into your entire being.
Recognize, celebrate and savor the feeling of being truly grateful for all you have been given.

Keep a gratitude journal to help rewire your brain to fire in more positive ways.
It doesn't get much better than this.

. . . . (• notes •) . . . .

30: here and now

• invocation

> let us give thanks for this day
> for new opportunities
> for new life and clear vision
>
> above us sky
> beneath us earth
> within us spirit
>
> feel the presence, power, and radiance of spirit
> as a great stream of slowly moving soft light
> filling our bodies
> filling this room
> filling all life with life
>
> feel the compulsion of spirit to manifest
> putting you, putting each of us, on the spot
>
> use the tremendous resources available to you
> here and now
> to create the finest relationships
> in all ways beholding the Divine
>
> feel the presence, power, and radiance of spirit
> as a great stream of grace
> filling all life with life

. . . . (• meditation •) . . . .

• blessing

> around us is creation ever-changing
> within us is spirit ever-flowing
> feel how blessed you are
> here and now
>
> and let us fill today with blessings
> let us bless one another and give thanks for the love and support we share
> let us bless our work and offer thanks to all the beings that are helping us
> and let us bless our planet, seeing it bathed in a streaming sphere of soft light
> an ever expanding flow of love
>
> hold a joyful vision of the garden of earth
> blossoming in peace and plenty
> here and now - right here and right now

30: here and now

Around us creation is ever-changing.

I walked out into a glorious sunset. My heart soared and I knew indisputably
that I was part of an ocean of infinite creativity and incandescent love.

I felt my speck-ness and my vast-ness simultaneously.
It felt like the first sunset.

Then suddenly it was gone replaced by a canopy of twinkling aliveness
and endless love.

Keep opening up to wilder and wider fields of possibility and perspective.
Keep looking up.

. . . . (• notes •) . . . .

31: into the new

• invocation

> we greet one another this morning by remembering
> there is but one life and we are living it
>
> with every breath our souls meet
> and spirit relates directly to and through us
>
> let it happen
>
> allow the contact to be made
>
> alliance with the highest means letting go
> of outdated beliefs and fancy trappings
> and moving courageously into the new
>
> into the now
> into the open
> into the unknown
> into the arms of love
>
> nothing less will see our planetary soul safely birthed

. . . . (• meditation •) . . . .

• blessing

> we are moving surely and steadily into the fulfillment of the new
>
> we see the light of spirit shining
> within ourselves
> within each another
>
> shining forth a message of love, understanding, gratitude and joy
>
> let it shine . . . . . shine out clear and radiant
> becoming stronger as it links with other points of light around our planet
> and the earth is truly blessed this morning
> and so are we all

31: into the new

Fortunately you are in the perfect position right now to

open your heart and your arms to life

say yes to what's happening

and

allow love to do its thing.

. . . . (• notes •) . . . .

32: let spirit flow

• invocation

let us give thanks for the spirit
that fills us and fills our lives
that draws us up and draws us out
and links us together
and lets us see who we are

our lives are filled with spirit
as we look back over today's events
let us recognize spirit flowing through the many moments, the many forms

let us see ourselves and our interactions from the highest point of view
if you were a soul what would you see?
what would today look like?

see all that has been accomplished
see new patterns that are emerging
and let your being rest in the light of this vision and be filled with gratitude
for all you are being given

for all you are being shown

. . . . (• meditation •) . . . .

• blessing

here is your present . . . a life on earth
here is your task . . . let spirit flow . . . unimpeded

live at the height of your consciousness

constant . . . steady . . . spontaneous . . .

and let us share our spirit with the universe
let your knowing, love, and gratitude stream out from this gathering
embracing the hearts of all

infusing and revitalizing the earth with spiritual light

let spirit flow

32: let spirit flow

See yourself as the soul looking back over today's events.
Describe what you see.

• *What opportunities were offered to you today?*

• *To what extent did you let spirit flow freely?*

• *What can you do differently tomorrow that will allow your spirit to flow unimpeded?*

. . . . (• notes •) . . . .

33: our hearts speak

• invocation

    the silence of our being together is rich
    within it let us give thanks for today

    for new opportunities
    for new life

    hold still
    hold fast

    stand firm
    stand steady

    i need you pure
    i need you free
    i need you all

    pure
    free
    united

    there is no other way for us to be together

    listen to the whisperings of your heart
    allow its wisdom to inspire and guide you

. . . . (• meditation •) . . . .

• blessing

    the silence of our being together is rich
    within it our hearts speak loud and clear

    let limitless love, truth and joy move through your open heart and out into the world now

    creating a network of goodness and kindness
    that soothes, nurtures and blesses all beings

33: our hearts speak

listen to the whisperings of your heart
allow its wisdom to inspire and guide you

Take a few moments to pause and drop into your heart center. Rest there for a while breathing slowly and deeply. Invite your heart to release any constrictions or stagnation and open even more.

Allow what you're feeling without making a story out of it.

Breathe in connectedness and breathe out gratitude from your softened open heart. As the breath flows in and out ask your heart to speak to you. Gently hold the intention that you want your heart to express itself. Simply sit, pay attention and notice how you feel. Give your live heart stream a chance. Let go and listen closely ...

When you open your eyes, look around and silently honor all the objects, plants, animals or people that may be present.

When you love without holding back or holding on,
know that your heart is speaking loud and clear.

. . . . (• notes •) . . . .

34: voyage into light

- invocation

>the ship is sailing
>it is sailing and we are on it
>
>every conscious joyous act of faith maintains buoyancy and keeps the ship afloat
>every act of faith that is pure, cuts cleanly through the waters of life, maintains direction
>and helps to transport this ship, this ark, earthwards onto new shores
>
>i am with you all
>i am within you all
>i am within the very structure of this boat
>i am the rudder and I am steering this ship to its appointed place
>
>there will be a navigator who will know the direction to take
>i will be working through him
>there will be a helmsman who will steer and I will be working though the helmsman
>i will be working through the captain
>i will be working through the cooks
>i am working within and through each one of you who is part of this vessel
>it is my vessel and I will guide it
>let me guide you
>
>look forward
>keep your focus on the constant horizon
>do all that is necessary to keep your vision clear
>
>be not concerned about the weather
>this is my ship whether the days be stormy or sunny
>know that the tempest is of me
>know that the fair-weather days are of me
>and that throughout all your days I am the energy
>that is moving you safely and surely towards your appointed destiny
>
>i name this ship The New Jerusalem
>blessed is this voyage carrying the faithful sailors home

. . . . (• meditation •) . . . .

- blessing

>we are creating a golden vessel of right action and love
>
>inner acts of faith are being translated into outer acts of friendship
>and we are the interpreters
>
>it requires us to do what we are doing
>to create open, clear communication between us
>and so release a unifying healing impulse of love
>that can empower and support the voyage of this planet into the light

34: voyage into light

The truth is that the ship is sailing and you are on it.

- Recall a time when your personality was radiant with faith.
- Remember the feeling of faith you had at that time along with the insight it brought you.
- As you awaken this memory from the past, bring it into your heart now.
- Allow faith to permeate through your life and radiate in all directions.

Keep your focus on the constant horizon.
Do all that is necessary to keep your vision clear.

Let faith hold your journey and trust it is carrying you where you need to be.

. . . . (• notes •) . . . .

35: we are here to love

• invocation

> pioneers
> we are here to love
>
> loving ourselves and each other
> means facing life with the courageous vulnerability of a warrior
>
> it means opening ourselves to the pain of self-confrontation
> and the joy of self-care and realization
>
> it means committing ourselves to conquering our own internal fears
> so we can move into life open without resistance
> to all that comes to us
>
> to bluff or lie to ourselves no longer works
> for this universe that we are a part of is scrupulously fair and responsive
>
> shedding guilts and fears and becoming visible
> we discover the strength to hold on to our center
> and let go of ourselves
>
> to kindness
> to joy
> to peace
> to clarity, wonder and more . . . to love

. . . . (• meditation •) . . . .

• blessing

> we are here to love
>
> open your heart
> think adventurously
> act joyously
>
> be gentle, appreciative, and supportive
> and, with an open heart, be firm, exacting, and honest
> and create relationships that in all ways give satisfaction and awareness to each other
>
> we are here to love
>
> let the light of this affirmation
> let the light of this action shine through you today
>
> let us love one another and in so doing
> revitalize our human family and expand the realm of spirit on earth

Deepening the Sacred . . .

35: we are here to love

I am here to love.

* Make this your affirmation of grace and gratitude this week.

* Affirm your intention, focus your attention, and choose love moment
  to moment.

* Stay focused. Stay with love and nothing else.

* Allow love to flow out as your energetic signature. Vibrate the love of God
  and essence of aliveness without qualification. Focus on what is streaming
  from your heart and create new pathways that allow love to do what it needs
  to do.

* Give your heart and soul over to the care of God and intuitively let anything
  other than the emerging divine impulse drop away.

. . . . (• notes •) . . . .

36: with each breath

• invocation

    we appreciate this morning the miracle of life
    the breath of spirit
    that streams through the galaxy
    and moves freely within us
    whose sweetness fills our beings

    it is the breath that has no ending
    it is the rhythm that never dies
    it is the presence that never leaves
    it is the love that enfolds us always

    i honor this day the breath of life
    the presence of love in me
    the presence of love in all I see

    with each breath
    I honor this presence

. . . . (• meditation •) . . . .

• blessing

    we breathe

    we breathe
    and as we do the universe breathes through us
    linking us together

    drawing us upwards, drawing us outwards

    we breathe and with each breath
    we bring kindness, goodness, and spaciousness to life
    we build presence

    with each breath
    we affirm our gratitude for a journey that engages the best in us

    and strengthens the best in the world

    with each breath
    we honor and build the presence that is love

Deepening the Sacred . . .

36: with each breath

A few slow, generous breaths always calms the body, expands it, and allows us to settle into the body so we can recognize the presence of love.

With each breath smile into your lungs.
Appreciate the joy of breathing fully and freely.

With each breath honor the aliveness in yourself and all you see.

. . . . (• notes •) . . . .

Beyond Our Lines
(best read out loud)

This is what I want to do
This is exactly how I want to live my life
Consciously taking risks and having a good time doing it
Expanding my total presence without embarrassment or denial of my power,
    Your power, our power, Divine power in this moment.
Putting everything right out here on the line
And then daring to really be myself.
Choosing to step beyond the lines I know and love so well
And deliberately risk everything I've built up this far to keep myself comfortable.
Not just once a workshop, once a week or once a day
But over and over and over
    Again and again
Until I experience my full potential
As a soul, as a teacher, as a woman, as a transformer.

I want to live this life - my life - to the fullest
And continually stretch and relax my boundaries out to include 'more'.
Amongst other things I want to experience an unplanned moment
An unpremeditated, unanticipated, unexpected, uncontrived, uncontrolled moment.
And, when it happens, I want to recognize it
Let go, open to it
And release my pictures of what *the* successful moment looks like
And of how I should perform within that moment
And simply surrender and trust my unknown abilities
And let my spirit rush into that space and show itself
Fully, authentically, magically, miraculously, splendidly, wonder-fully ... the works!

And I want to be substantially different as a result
I expect that moment to make a difference to the rest of my life
And I want there to be a difference in the world because of the choices made
    In that single moment
And, since I don't know when that moment's coming,
I want to experience all moments as possible entry points - just in case this is IT
And stay conscious and be present to myself, to you, to what's happening now
    Within me and between us - along with all the possibilities of what can happen next.
I want to see clearly whatever's going on and respond to it.

And I don't want to feel like I'm doing this on my own
I want friends to help.
I want to feel close and touched, loved and empowered by God's living grace - you folks.
So that together we can celebrate our full power as women making a difference
Together we can celebrate our full power as men making a difference
And together we can apply our spiritual passion for life
And build a planet of light and transformation which really works

Within our lifetimes.

Afterword

A new consciousness is emerging.
It is fresh, spontaneous, alive!

Welcome what arises in each moment.
Give it your best.

Live with intention.

Index of First Lines

allow yourself to open 62

appreciate your divine attributes 46

as individuals we hold a beautiful vision 28

as we welcome this day 4

become aware of the presence of the divine 12

become aware of your location 14

behold the world with soul sight 54

give yourself fully to the process of creation 24

how can you assist planetary transformation? 44

how far does your commitment extend? 16

in the peace and quiet at the end of the day * 64

let us awaken to the gift of today 2

let us give thanks for the spirit * 70

let us give thanks for this day 66

life force 26

life is a pilgrimage 8

lift yourself out of ignorance 32

listen 10

our pledge to spirit is total 48

paradise 50

pioneers 76

the heart is open 56

there is a presence here 36

the ship is sailing 74

the silence of our being together is rich 72

we appreciate this morning the miracle of life 78

we are all enrolled in a spiritual school 6

we are each a gift to the other 38

we are each involved 30

we are here to manifest love 58

we are infinite beings discovering our finiteness 18

we greet one another this morning by remembering 68

what's involved in living a spiritual life? 22

where is love? 42

within this room 34

you are a landing pad for grace 52

* evening prayer

ABOUT THE PUBLISHER

Lorian Press is a private, for profit business which publishes works approved by the Lorian Association. Current titles can be found on the Lorian website www.lorian.org.

The Lorian Association is a not-for-profit educational organization. Its work is to help people bring the joy, healing, and blessing of their personal spirituality into their everyday lives. This spirituality unfolds out of their unique lives and relationships to Spirit, by whatever name or in whatever form that Spirit is recognized. For more information, go to www.lorian.org.

MORE PRAISE FOR *SOUL INFUSIONS*

"I enjoy how applicable *Soul Infusions* is to my life. The words are simple and poignant. The layout of the book makes it easy to read."
  Cindy Dollar - Owner One Center Yoga Studio, Certified Iyengar Yoga Instructor

"In *Soul Infusions*, Joy Drake has lovingly shaped a chalice of inspired meditations that invite us daily into the sanctuary of our human divinity. Each meditation offers a unique pathway to explore the landscape of the soul, its beauty and boundlessness, and each is accompanied by practical exercises that apply the gifts of our souls to our everyday lives, infusing them with love, power, and kindness. Based on forty years of devoted spiritual practice by a master of soul alchemy, this little book is a classic of soul in service to the Sacred, in service to our world."
  Hiro Boga - Writer, Teacher, Mentor

CPSIA information can be obtained
at www.ICGtesting.com
Printed in the USA
FFOW02n0704281015
18093FF

9 780936 878690